NEXT:

Four Steps to Get Unstuck and Walk Into Purpose

Dorenthea Nemeth

Unless otherwise indicated, Scriptures are taken from the King James Version (KJV).

Scripture quotations marked NKJV taken from the New King James Version®. Copyright © 1982 by Thomas Nelson. Used by permission. All rights reserved.

Scripture quotations marked NIV are taken from the Holy Bible, New International Version®, NIV®. Copyright © 1973, 1978, 1984, 2011 by Biblica, Inc.™ Used by permission of Zondervan. All rights reserved worldwide. www.zondervan.com The "NIV" and "New International Version" are trademarks registered in the United States Patent and Trademark Office by Biblica, Inc.™

Scripture quotations marked NLT are taken from the Holy Bible, New Living Translation, Copyright ©1996, 2004, 2007, 2013, 2015 by Tyndale House Foundation. Used by permission of Tyndale House Publishers, Inc., Carol Stream, Illinois 60188. All rights reserved.

Scripture quotations marked CEV are from the Contemporary English Version Copyright © 1991, 1992, 1995 by American Bible Society. Used by Permission.

Scripture quotations taken from THE MESSAGE, copyright © 1993, 1994, 1995, 1996, 2000, 2001, 2002 by Eugene H. Peterson. Used by permission of

NavPress. All rights reserved. Represented by Tyndale House Publishers, Inc.

Scripture quotations taken from the New American Standard Bible® (NASB), Copyright © 1960, 1962, 1963, 1968, 1971, 1972, 1973, 1975, 1977, 1995 by The Lockman Foundation. Used by permission.
www.Lockman.org

Unless otherwise indicated, definitions are taken from the Merriam-Webster Dictionary.

I dedicate this book to my awesome and amazing husband, Albert, who God made just for me, to love me when I'm unlovable and to be patient with me when I'm impatient.

Thank you for believing in me more than I believe in myself.

I love you!

Contents

Introduction 1

Step One
Leave the Past Behind: He's Doing a New Thing 6
1. RUN AFTER GOD, FIRST 7
2. A NEW THING 13
3. WHAT YOU LOOKIN' AT? 19

Step Two
Stop & Retreat 23
4. STOP MAJORING IN THE MINORS 25
5. STOP TRYING TO DO IT ALONE 33
6. ARE YOU LISTENING? 39
7. IT'S NOT ALL ABOUT YOU 47

Step Three
Get In Position 52
8. POSITION YOURSELF 53
9. SPEAK TO IT! 61
10. THERE'S POWER IN YOUR PRAISE 71
11. YOUR ANSWER IS IN HIS PRESENCE 81

Step Four
Embrace Your NEXT 86
    12. IT'S TIME TO DREAM AGAIN 87
    13. INCREASE YOUR VALUE 93
    14. WISE STEWARDSHIP 101
    15. WALK INTO YOUR NEXT 109
    Conclusion 117
    Endnotes 119

Introduction

As common as it may seem, we all fall sometimes. It is God's desire for us to look to Him for guidance in our decisions, and in every problem we may face. However, we fail—in our humanity—to reach out, displaying our imperfection. We serve a mighty God who knows us better than we know ourselves, and as we yield to Him, He'll take us by the hand and take us to that place we were supposed to be all along—to our NEXT.

Why do we fear? Why won't we pray? Is it because of what He'll tell us, we may not want to hear what He has to say, or do what He asks us to do? As we are obedient to God, He assures us in His word that He'll never leave or forsake us.

Then, what is it that keeps us from drawing close to Him?

We often walk in a world of "unknowns", not knowing what tomorrow has in store. God said in Isaiah 55 that His ways are not our ways, neither are His thoughts our thoughts; for as high as the heavens are above the sea, so are His ways higher than our ways, and His thoughts higher than our thoughts. My friend, be encouraged knowing that we serve an all-knowing God. He's powerful, and nothing that happens in our lives takes Him by surprise.

As we go through life, many question, "God, if you're here, why is this happening to me? Don't you care?" And, of course, though we know He cares, it sure does feel like He doesn't.

Don't you know that God knows what's best for you? That He has a plan for you that is so phenomenal, that if you knew what it was, you couldn't handle it? It's so big, it would blow your mind! That's the kind of God we serve. He's a God of the impossible. There's nothing that He can't do. Though it seems that you're all alone, you're never alone. What you're going through right now is a time of pruning; a time of watering; a time of growing.

Like a plant, we have to be pruned sometimes. God is stripping some things, or people, away from our lives. Things and people, that over a period of time, will do us more harm than good. They can be deadly. He wants nothing but the best for us, because He loves us, but it can hurt so bad to say goodbye to those things, habits or people that will do nothing but destroy us in the end. But we should always remember Romans 8:28. No matter how bad it hurts, it's working for your good.

Picture it like this, imagine in your mind a block of clay that has yet to be shaped and molded. The artist has to chip away at the clay in order to get it to its desired form.

The artist is chipping away the imperfections. And like that artist, God chips away at us to cut off the excess baggage that we carry around in our lives, which keep us back from possessing the life that He has for us.

There are some things from which we have to be delivered that only He can do. Possibly things that are strongholds, which left to our own selves and our own devices, we can't let them go, no matter how hard we try. You have to relinquish control—surrender.

Yes, surrender. That's not a word most of us like. We all like to be in control. We want to win, no matter the cost. Even if it means hurting someone else, or even ourselves, in the process.

The word "surrender" is actually a process in itself. It takes time to surrender, to finally say, "Okay, Lord, I tried it my way, and my way isn't getting it done. Your turn now." Yes, for some of us, we have to wait until we've made a big mess of things before we're just ready to give up. Then God in His infinite love and patience just sighs and says, "Finally!"

Have you ever wondered what life would be like if you just surrendered everything to God? What it would be like to never worry about anything or fear anything? It is possible to have everything your heart desires and live life abundantly. It's all in our surrender.

Well, if it was that easy, then why don't we have it? Like I just said, we want to be in control.

I'm reminded of a time I didn't have peace in my marriage. Whenever my husband, Albert, and I had a disagreement, I would try to use the word of God to manipulate him and try to get him to see things my way. Did it work? NO! Then, the Holy Spirit finally let me know (or maybe I finally decided to listen) that I can't change him. Only God can change him. It's up to me to pray for him and love him, unconditionally, whether or not he did what I wanted him to do or behaved how I wanted him to be behave. And, wow, once I listened to the Holy Spirit and stopped arguing with Albert, the peace that I felt, and continue to feel, is awesome. Why? Because I surrendered.

We want to rule the world. Have everything go our way, and life would just be perfect, right? WRONG! When God created Adam and Eve, they were created for worship. And then we all know the story of their disobedience and the disobedience of mankind ever since.

Now we live in a world that forces us to work by the sweat of our brow. A world of pain and sorrow. A world of worry and fear. That was never God's original plan. But the Bible says that though we are in the world, we are not of the world. We are children of God.

As children of God, we have access to very special benefits. One of those benefits is peace, for example, no matter what is going on in our lives. Total peace, freedom from worry, is just one of the many benefits and blessings that God has for us. There is so much more He has for you!

We can't control people. And sometimes, we can't control the things that happen in our lives. Sometimes life just happens. But we can control how we respond to the challenges that life brings our way. Will you respond in anger, bitterness, and unforgiveness, or will you respond in peace? Will you complain, or will you surrender to the hand of God upon your life? We have many weapons and keys that our Father has granted us to overcome the enemy and the problems we encounter. It's up to us whether or not we utilize those keys.

The keys you will read about in this book have been stepping stones in my own life. I have used them to bring me into the abundant life that I now possess and the abundant life that God promises in His Word for you. Each chapter will give you insight into getting unstuck, living on purpose and possessing everything He has for you. This is your time and your season. Are you ready to unlock the doors of abundant living and live on purpose every day of your life? Then read on, because your time is now!

Step One

Leave the Past Behind:
He's Doing a New Thing

One

RUN AFTER GOD, FIRST

Hear, O Israel: The Lord our God, the Lord is one. Love the Lord your God with all your heart and with all your soul and with all your strength.
Deuteronomy 6:4-5 (NIV)

What does it mean to love God? For me, it means having such adoration for Him that to live without Him is worse than death. Because, if truth be told, without God, we are dead--spiritually. That's worse than natural death. I've been in church all my life, so it's very hard for me to imagine my life without Christ.

I don't understand how people call themselves followers of Christ, yet, don't spend time with Him. They go to church on Sunday, but curse, drink, etc., Monday through Saturday, basically doing their own thing. Then, we come to church and wonder why our services are dead. The fact is, it's hard to have a spiritually ALIVE church with spiritually DEAD people.

Sometimes, when I'm leading worship in my church and the people are just standing (or sitting) there with no emotion, watching us sing and praise God, I just want to yell, "Come on y'all! Get it together! Wake up!"

I know that one of my life's assignments is to lead God's people into His presence through praise and worship. But something that I had to learn a long time ago is, you can't take people where they don't want to go. I can sing song after song. I can be anointed. I can fast and pray. I can cry and sweat. But if the people in the congregation don't do their part, and by that I mean, love God with their praise and worship, then I sometimes feel that all my tears and sweat are in vain. However, something that God revealed to me is that things aren't always as they appear. Though it may not look like it, somebody is being blessed. Even if it's just one person, somebody is getting it.

In John 14:15, Jesus told his disciples, "If you love me, keep my commands." To love God means to obey Him.

My children are grown now, but when they were younger, I required obedience from them. In my home, Albert and I have always practiced telling our children we love them. So, they have no problem telling us they love us when they feel the urge. However, if my son or daughter told me they loved me, but they never did anything I told them to do, then I would have reason to believe that they really didn't love me. Why? Because they didn't do what I asked.

It's the same thing with God. We can't say we love Him, but yet don't do what He says. I put this chapter first, because the first step to receiving everything God has for you is (and excuse my English), you gotta love Him. And more than that, you gotta obey Him.

The Israelites are a prime example of disobedience. So many times they disobeyed God. In the Old Testament, we witness how one king after another disobeyed God, and because of their disobedience, God allowed them to be defeated by their enemies. They never did possess everything God had for them.

What was the last thing God asked you to do, but you still haven't done it? How many times has our disobedience prevented us from walking in the fullness of God's blessings?

Our first example of disobedience in the Bible is none other than Adam and Eve. After God created them, he put them in a garden, the Garden of Eden. It was paradise, a place where God lived and talked with them. They had everything they could ever want or need. They could do whatever they wanted to do, with one stipulation. They could not eat of the tree of the knowledge of good and evil. But of course, Satan being as sly as he was, convinced them to do otherwise. Hence, the fall of man. You know the story.

They were thrown out of the Garden of Eden, all because for a brief moment, their love went from God to themselves. They loved themselves, and wanted to please themselves, more than God.

To love God may sound like a simple thing to do. But because of the fallen state of mankind, to love God, to really and truly love God, isn't that easy for some. It's easier to do things our own way, to love ourselves and things, rather than God. To love God means to be intimate with Him. It means to desire Him more than your next breath. To obey Him, even if it means going against the norm.

The greatest example of love is Jesus. Again, you know the story of how he came to die for us. Who else in this world loves you so much that they would be willing to die for you?

Before I go up before the congregation to sing, I have to first examine my heart. I have to make sure there's no disobedience or unrepentant sin in my life. Disobedience, or sin, separates us from not only His blessings, but His presence. If I don't have anything else in the world, I MUST have His presence.

Some people only love God when He's pouring out His blessings in their lives. Then, at the first sign of trouble or a problem, they run to everything and everyone else, but God. They run to that person or thing or food that makes them feel good. They run to the familiar.

I want to encourage you to take that first step—love God with all your heart, soul and strength. Only then will you begin to see and walk in the fullness of His love and blessings and purpose for your life. Yes, God has a plan and a purpose for you. Worship Him. Obey Him. And watch His plan unfold before your very eyes.

Two

A NEW THING

Remember ye not the former things, neither consider the things of old. Behold, I will do a new thing; now it shall spring forth; shall ye not know it? I will even make a way in the wilderness, and rivers in the desert.
Isaiah 43:19

This verse is one of my favorite scriptures. Especially when God says, "Behold, I will do a new thing..." Sometimes, we get stuck in the "former things"—the past. We can't let go of old habits, old ways of thinking and doing things. I feel in my spirit to say to you right now, "Let it go!" The time is over for regrets. God has a plan for your today, for your tomorrow. The following examples are situations that keep us stuck, afraid to walk into that new thing that God has for us:

- That old boyfriend that keeps hurting you, and deep down inside, you know he is not the one. But you keep holding on to him because you're scared of being alone.

- You're unhappy at your job, but don't want to go anywhere else because of the security your current job gives you.

- You know you need to go back to school to get your degree, but won't do it because of the fear of how hard it'll be or how old you are.

- You've been hanging around the same friends who don't seem to be adding to your well-being, but they're draining you instead. Yet, you still hang out with them, because it's too hard to make new friends.

- You've been wanting to ask for a raise or promotion for the longest time, but won't do it because of fear of losing your job.

It is time for you to possess everything God has for you. Don't be afraid of the new thing. God has a new man, a new job, a new career, and new friends waiting for you. But He can't give it to you until you forget the former things. In other words, God can't bless you with the new until you let go of the old.

I just want to take a minute to talk to you about the people in your life who were only meant to be in your life for a season, but you have let them overstay their welcome because you didn't want to hurt their feelings. A lot times, it's the people we hang around that keep us stuck and they hinder us from walking into our purpose. They call themselves your friend, but when you're around them, they never have anything positive to say. Let them go! They were just meant to be in your life for a season. That season is over! I was listening to video by the late Dr. Myles Munroe and he said:

If you are in a group and you're the smartest in the group, it's time to leave the group. You don't want to be in a group that can't grow you, expand you and improve you. You need to do an inventory of your friends and the people you hang around.1

Your relationships should be assets, not deficits. The people in your life should add value to you, not take value away from you by causing you to speak or act in ways that decrease your value. God wants to bring you into a new season. A season of freshness and wholeness.

Many times we miss the direction and leading of the Holy Spirit because our pipes are clogged, for lack of a better word. You know how the pipes in your house get clogged up with hair or food, which in turn makes it hard for the water to get through or go down?

God has wisdom and revelation that He wants to pour down into your spirit to get you to that next level. But He can't because your mind and spirit are clogged up with so much junk, that nothing else can get in.

If you can, you just need to close your eyes right now and take a deep breath. Tell God, "Father, please help me get the junk out."

"Well, how do I do this," you may ask. It requires submission. That means that you may have to say no to some people or things that keep you from reaching your goals and dreams. This may mean saying no to yourself. Your flesh wants a lot of things that really aren't bad, but they're not good for you, for this season in your life.

Submitting means saying yes to God. Some of you are afraid to say yes because of the cost. You want God to do something new, something greater in your life, but you feel that the cost is too high. But He even made a provision for that. I love God because once you say yes, He makes it easy for you. Notice that in Isaiah 43:19, God said, "…I will even make a way in the wilderness, and rivers in the desert." In other words, even in your hardest times, your driest times, He will make a way. So, you see? You don't have to do it alone. He won't ask you to do anything that He hasn't already equipped you for.

When Albert came home from prison five years ago, my children and I were living in a nice apartment in a good neighborhood in Rochester, Michigan. However, once the state found out that Albert, an ex-convict on probation (at the time) was living there, the parole office basically evicted us from Michigan, and told us that we had to move back to Toledo, where Albert was convicted. Talk about a blow to our faith!

We didn't know where we were going to go. One day we drove to Toledo to look at some homes to rent that we could afford. It's funny now, but at the time, it was anything but funny. Albert literally cried after we saw some of the homes and neighborhoods in our price range. It bothered him so much to think about uprooting his wife and children from a gorgeous, affluent area to a place that looked like a slum. It was bad!

Instead, we decided to get out of debt first and wait until we had the money for a down payment for a home in a good neighborhood that met our standards. I'm so glad that God gave us the wisdom to wait. However, this meant that Albert would have to leave me and the kids temporarily (again), and he would live with some close friends of ours who lived in Toledo.

He was ordered not to come back to Michigan until he was off probation. But, on the weekends, he would sneak into Michigan anyway so that we could be together, if even for only a few hours. Fortunately, this only lasted for around five months. It wasn't long because the Lord made "a way in the wilderness". And now we have a beautiful home and we tell everybody, "God did it."

It wasn't easy. I had to leave my job. Our children hated it because they had to leave their friends. But, God is faithful. He blessed Albert with a good job, me with another job and the kids made new friends.

Isaiah 1:19 says, "If you are willing and obedient, you will eat the fat (good things) of the land." Obedience is key. Don't believe the lie of the enemy. You're in the right place at the right time for God to do something new in your life--when you submit to Him and His way.

You may be in a wilderness or a dry place in your life right now. Let God come in and drench your dry places. He wants to do a new thing in you, through you and for you.

Three

WHAT YOU LOOKIN' AT?

"...and that the LORD may keep his promise to me: 'If your descendants watch how they live, and if they walk faithfully before me with all their heart and soul, you will never fail to have a successor on the throne of Israel.'"
1 Kings 2:4

The above scripture included some of David's last words to his son, Solomon, before he died and left Solomon the throne. David was letting Solomon know that as long as he remained obedient to the Lord, God would take care of the rest. And we have that same promise in Matthew 6:33, which tells us to seek God first. In other words, put Him first and do what He wants, then He'll take care of the rest.

Something that I've learned to do lately is change my perspective. I can't remember now where I read it, but it was an article about how our perspective determines our feelings, whether we feel good or bad about something. So, lately, instead of focusing on the negative part of a situation, I'm learning to look at the positive side of things. When I lead our worship service, I no longer focus on the people who aren't getting it. I focus on the ones who are.

You see, whenever something unfortunate occurs, the enemy always has a knack of getting us to focus on the negative part, and he'll totally blind us to the positive part, if we let him. It's such an easy trap that we often find ourselves falling into. Negative thoughts lead to sadness and depression. You then find yourself beating yourself up—over nothing.

When it comes to our past, we always focus on the coulda's, shoulda's and woulda's. "If I would have known, I woulda I done this." "I coulda done that." "I shoulda done this."

It's the enemy's desire to keep us living in regret. The past is done. You can't change it. Learn from it, even cry if you need to, and then move on. It's called the God factor. Without God, we can't do anything. But with God, we can do ALL things. It's not His desire for us to live in the past, full of regrets. Yes, you made some stupid mistakes back in the day. We all have. But now it's time to release it. Let it go. It's excess baggage and anything in excess is too much, and it can weigh you down. You have to get rid of the excess baggage.

One day during my study time, I was reading 1 Kings 2. David had just made Solomon king in the previous chapter and now David is getting ready to die. He wants to give his last will and testament, but there is some unfinished business. And sure enough, after he died, Solomon dealt with it.

There were some men David let get away with murder, literally. There were some men David encountered during his rulership that weren't good for him. One of them disobeyed David's orders, while another one just outright cursed David to his face right there in front of his men. Solomon wasted no time having these men annihilated. He knew that if he didn't do it to them first, they were going to do it to him. They were a threat to his future.

We have to deal with feelings of regret early on or they'll pose as threats to our future, keeping us from fulfilling God's plan for our lives.

A while ago while I was speaking at my brother's church, I used an analogy of me driving a car. When we drive, it's safe to look in our rearview mirror sometimes. As drivers, we should always be aware of everything that's going on around us, in front of us and on the side of us, while keeping an eye on that car behind us. But we can't always be looking in the rearview mirror, or we would crash. See where I'm going with this?

When moving forward in life, you have to look ahead to what's in front of you. If you're always looking back with shame and regrets, you won't get anywhere, or worse yet, you'll crash, possibly hurting other people, including yourself. Nothing good happens when we're always focusing on the past, constantly looking back.

Negative things happen in life. We sometimes make bad decisions along the way. I choose not to focus on the bad choices I've made, because out of everything negative that happened in my life, God was faithful. I can't help but quote Romans 8:28, "And we know that all things work together for good to them that love God, to them who are the called according to His purpose." God has been too good for us to wallow in self-pity and regret. For every negative thing that we could feel sorry for, there are 10 times as many things for which to give God glory and thanks. One thing I know for sure, He has never let me down. And He'll never let you down.

Step Two

Stop & Retreat

Four

STOP MAJORING IN THE MINORS

As Jesus and His disciples were on their way, He came to a village where a woman named Martha opened her home to Him. She had a sister called Mary, who sat at the Lord's feet listening to what He said. But Martha was distracted by all the preparations that had to be made. She came to Him and asked, "Lord, don't you care that my sister has left me to do the work by myself? Tell her to help me!" "Martha, Martha," the Lord answered, "You are worried and upset about many things, but few things are needed—or indeed only one. Mary has chosen what is better, and it will not be taken away from her."
Luke 10:38-42, CEV

In the above passage, we find two women who are sisters. One of them, Martha, appears to be the ideal woman, or super-woman, if you will. She's been to the market to buy all the ingredients to prepare this glorious meal for Jesus and His disciples. She labored and toiled in that hot kitchen for hours for what would be the "meal of the year". And, oh, what a grand meal it was—absolutely delicious! All the disciples complimented Martha telling her that she was the best cook in the world.

Now that everyone has eaten, are well satisfied, and have gathered into the living room, Jesus is getting ready to pour himself out as he ministers to them with His words. He's getting ready to feed their spirit man now, with spiritual food.

Martha is busy clearing the table and washing the dishes. Heaven forbid she leaves the kitchen a mess with a sink full of dishes to clean, while Jesus is sitting in the living room speaking words from heaven itself.

Mary, on the other hand is sitting at the feet of Jesus taking in His every word. She was not going to miss this opportunity of a lifetime!

However, Martha didn't think it was an opportunity of a lifetime—and she made it known. She actually told Jesus in Luke 10:40, "'Lord, doesn't it bother you that my sister has left me to do all the work by myself? Tell her to come and help me!'"(CEV). But you have to love Jesus' patient and soft rebuke in verse 41, "'Martha, Martha, you are worried and troubled about many things. But one thing is needed, and Mary has chosen that good part, which will not be taken away from her.'"

How could Martha miss it? The same way you and I miss it—all the time. I think it's two reasons. The first reason being that we are so busy, we let ourselves get distracted or turned away from the "needful thing"—the presence of God. Oh, to be in His presence. Psalm 16:11 says,

"You will show me the path of life; In Your presence is fullness of joy; At Your right hand are pleasures forevermore" (NKJV).

If only we knew the blessings that come from being in His presence. Which brings me to the second reason why we miss it sometimes—lack of revelation. We lack revelation of who God is and what He's able to do in our lives. So, if the enemy can keep us from being in God's presence with busyness and distractions, being worried and troubled about many things, then the enemy has won. He knows that as long as we are distracted with the cares of life, we won't seek God. Seeking God brings revelation of who God is and His power. Once we know who God is and what He longs and desires to do for us, we will begin to walk in peace, favor and wisdom. All from being in His presence.

You may be wondering, "How do I get in His presence?" God has given us many ways to get into His presence. A few of these ways are studying His word, prayer, praise and worship. I don't know what I would do if I didn't have God. And I am so glad that because of Jesus and His death on the cross, we have access to our heavenly Father 24 hours a day, seven days a week. We don't have to wait until Sunday to experience God and the peace that only He can give. I don't know about you, but I NEED His presence. There's a yearning in me to constantly seek Him in His word and in worship. And when you seek

Him, having peace is easy. Drugs and the other substances that the world uses to have peace, only last a few short hours. Those things are just counterfeits of the real thing. There is no peace like the peace of God. Matthew 13:1-8 says:

> Then He spoke many things to them in parables, saying: "Behold, a sower went out to sow. And as he sowed, some seed fell by the wayside; and the birds came and devoured them. Some fell on stony places, where they did not have much earth; and they immediately sprang up because they had no depth of earth. But when the sun was up they were scorched, and because they had no root they withered away. And some fell among thorns, and the thorns sprang up and choked them. But others fell on good ground and yielded a crop: some a hundredfold, some sixty, some thirty.

Later in the chapter, Jesus explains what this parable means. I want to focus on the seed that "fell among the thorns." Jesus says that these particular seeds represent the people who hear the word, but "the cares of this world and the deceitfulness of riches choke the word, and he becomes unfruitful."

John 16:33 says, "These things I have spoken to you, that in Me you may have peace. In the world you will have tribulation; but be of good cheer, I have overcome the world." Some of you may think, "Humph! That's easy for Jesus to say. Has he seen my bills? Has he seen how these people treat me on my job? Did he hear the doctor last week when she told me that I have cancer? And that's not the half of it. Does Jesus know everything I have to do? I have to work. Then, I have to come home to these spoiled kids and cook them something to eat and help them with their homework. I have no time for myself. Then, I have to get up the next morning and do it all over again. Be of good cheer?!? Yeah, right!"

This, my friend, is what Jesus meant when he was referring to the cares of this world. That's what Martha's problem was. She was more concerned about having a clean house, than resting in His presence. I can just hear the Spirit beckoning, saying, "Come to me, all you who labor and are heavy laden, and I will give you rest." He's commanding us to come to Him. It doesn't get any plainer than that.

Say this prayer aloud if you can, "Father, I'm sorry for the times you called me into your presence to rest, but I ignored you. Forgive me, Lord. Help me to answer your call, to stop doing what I'm doing, and to run into your presence so that I may receive your peace and every wonderful blessing that comes from being in your presence. In Jesus's Name, Amen."

Let's look at the word peace for a moment. According to the Merriam-Webster Dictionary, peace is, "a state of tranquility or quiet." But the peace I'm referring to is so much more than that. Peace, or some derivative form of peace, is in the Bible 397 times. That's a lot of peace. Actually, Jesus is called the "Prince of Peace" in Isaiah 9:6.

The Hebrew word for peace is shalom. And when you consider the meaning of shalom, peace means so much more than tranquility or quietness. It means harmony, wholeness, completeness, prosperity, well-being, and so much more. All of that wrapped up in one word. And that's what our Father wants to give you. But you cannot, and will not attain true peace any other way, except in His presence.

We have to make a choice that we will not be more concerned about this world and all it has to offer, such as riches and fame, than we are about our relationship with the living God. He lovingly longs to pour His love, peace and joy upon us, but we miss it. What we have to do and what is on our agenda is more important. It must hurt as a father, who has the answer to everything we will ever go through, to stand by waiting for us to come to Him, but yet we refuse to go to Him.

If you're a parent, then I'm sure you can relate. Imagine your son or daughter going through a dilemma. You have the answer, but they refuse to speak to you or come tell you about it. Or maybe they come to you and you give them advice, but they refuse to take it. They'd rather do it their way, because of course to them, their way is better. Then, because they refused to come to you or listen to your words of wisdom, things just got worse. Now, they're crying, hurt and depressed. And you're hurting, because that's your baby, because no matter how old they get, they'll always be your baby. And to think, if only they would've come to you and taken your advice, how things would've turned out so differently.

Get in His presence. Don't wait another day. Then, don't let another day go by without spending some time with Him. Let Him hold you. Let Him love you. Let Him fill you. Let Him lift you. Psalm 3:3 says, "But You, O LORD, are a shield for me, my glory and the One who lifts up my head."

Five

STOP TRYING TO DO IT ALONE

No weapon that is formed against you shall prosper; and every tongue that shall rise against thee in judgment thou shalt condemn.
Isaiah 54:17

Just recently, I noticed that many times in the Bible, the enemies of the people of God ended up killing themselves. Of course, it took the people of God doing their part, such as in 1 Samuel 14 when Jonathan and his armor bearer went to face the Philistines alone, believing that God would deliver the Philistines into their hands. And boy, did He deliver! God put the Philistines in confusion so that they killed each other.

Then, there's another instance in Judges 7 where God used Gideon and his 300 men to defeat the Midianite army. As Gideon and his men shouted, "'A sword for the LORD and for Gideon'… the LORD caused the Midianite army to turn on each other with their own swords."

I say all that to say this, don't worry about your enemies. The battle is not yours, but it belongs to the Lord. Give it to Him and watch Him fight for you. He's waiting for you to come to Him, and then let Him do the rest.

He didn't say that problems wouldn't come, but He did say they won't prosper. They won't succeed. The devil is out for your demise, but don't give up. Keep standing. Keep believing. God is not through with you yet. He has great and mighty things in store for you that your mind can't conceive. And it's the enemy's job to distract you. He knows that if he can distract you and get your eyes off of God and His Word, that's half the battle right there. You already have the victory. There is nothing that Satan can do to pluck you out of the hand of God. Now, you can willingly walk away, but as long as you want to be kept, the Lord will keep you.

Know that God will bring you out and the enemy you're facing today, you will see no more. While Moses was leading the children of Israel out of Egypt, Moses said, "Do not fear! Stand by and see the salvation of the LORD which He will accomplish for you today; for the Egyptians whom you have seen today, you will never see them again forever. The LORD will fight for you while you keep silent." (NASB)

Take note of that last sentence, "The LORD will fight for you while you keep silent." Your enemies may be talking about you and running your name in the ground, but if you will keep your mouth shut, the Lord will fight for you.

You may be going through the worst battle in your life right now, but God is fighting for you. Trouble may be coming in from every side, but God is fighting for you. Every lie that your enemy spoke against you will be proven to be wrong, because God is fighting for you.

Many times we're tempted to stand up for ourselves and try to convince people to be on our side. That's not your job. You're not your own, you belong to Jesus. Let him fight for you. No matter what you do, you can't please everybody, ALL the time. As children of God, our number one duty is to please Him, first and foremost. When you please Him, He will make your enemies your footstool.

There's an old school gospel song that says, "Victory, victory shall be mine! If I hold my peace, and let the Lord fight my battle, victory, victory shall be mine!" Yep! It's that easy. Hold your peace! Even when it looks like it's over, it's not over. God has the final say. He's able to turn any situation around. He's able to bring any dead situation back to life, if that's what you want Him to do.

Yes, sometimes it takes time. Did you know that your prayers are answered as soon as you pray? However, the answer may not always be what we want to hear at the time. Of course, we want Him to answer our prayers, our way—with a "Yes". But because He knows what's best for us, we may not receive that "yes" right now. Sometimes, His answer is "No" or "Wait". But when God says, "Now", you better watch out.

I remember after Albert had been in prison for 12 years already and it was December 2011. We were believing the Lord to answer our prayer that year, even though he still had four more years to go on a 16 year sentence—but our faith was high. Holy Spirit had already told Albert that he wouldn't have to serve the full sentence. So you can imagine my heartbreak at the end of 2011 and my husband still wasn't home.

Since it's the first day of a new year, January 1st is routinely acknowledged as the day of new beginnings or a fresh start, however, January 1, 2012 was one of the worst days of my life.

I was in the tub talking to Albert on the phone, crying, wondering why isn't Albert home with me and our children? God, what is taking you so long?!? Then, a few days passed and I got the call-- he was coming home.

I felt ashamed of myself. If only I had kept the faith for just a few more days. But who's to say, that maybe that breakdown moment I had in the tub was exactly what God was waiting for—for me to come to the end of myself, when there was NOTHING left to do, but trust Him.

Many times, we postpone our blessings with our mouths. Remember the scripture we just read, "The LORD will fight for you while you keep silent." This requires humility. It's hard to be quiet sometimes, isn't it, when you're being talked about and humiliated. Sometimes, we feel like we have to have the final word. You don't always have to have the final word. It's just a matter of time until the lies of the enemy will be blown up to pieces and fall to the ground. His lies will be rendered inoperative in your life. They carry no weight as far as you are concerned because you are a child of the King. So, stop your worrying, and start singing and praising God. We serve a mighty God. He'll never leave us or forsake us. He's always there, even when we can't see Him or feel Him.

We've become such a touchy-feely generation. If we can't see it or touch it or feel it, then it's not real. Faith is at an all-time low, while doubt and unbelief are at an all-time high. It's time for our generation to rise up in faith.

Lately, the Lord has been speaking to me about the signs, wonders and miracles in which we should be walking. But we aren't, because we don't have the faith that those old mothers had back in the day. When they wouldn't stop praying and fasting until what they were praying for came to pass. I want that faith. I want to see, but not only see, I want to be one of the ones that God uses to bring his miracles to pass on the earth. The things that once had my attention, don't have my attention anymore. God has birthed in me a hunger for more of Him. I'm tired of church as usual. I want to behold the signs and wonders today that we read about in the Bible. I'm chasing after Him like never before. It's our time to take back what the enemy stole.

Matthew 10:8 commissions us to do four things, "Heal the sick, raise the dead, cleanse those who have leprosy, drive out demons. Freely you have received; freely give." We have the power, now it's time to give it away.

Six

ARE YOU LISTENING?

And your ears shall hear a word behind you, saying, "This is the way, walk in it," when you turn to the right or when you turn to the left.
Isaiah 30:21

Yesterday, I decided to stop by McDonald's after my workout at the gym. (Don't judge.) Albert was on his way to a Harley Davidson meeting, so I decided that I'd get a burger and some fries (yes, McDonald's has the best fries) and I decided to just have some me-time.

Well, normally, I'll just go through the drive-thru and park the car and eat. But this time, for some strange reason, I wanted to go in and eat instead. So, I got out of the car, and before I could even get to the door, I looked inside and saw a young lady who used to attend my church and who I hadn't seen in a while. I should've known that God wanted me to go in for a reason.

I asked her why she hadn't been coming to church, and of course, she tried to make excuses. We talked for a while and I took her home and encouraged her to come back to church. I believe that the Lord wanted me to plant that little seed in this young lady to remind her of her need for Him.

Though this may be a small thing to some, it was a big deal to me. I was amazed. I thought that I was just going there to spend some time alone, by myself, and relax, but instead God sent me inside McDonald's for this young lady. He is always speaking. The question is, "Are we listening?"

We see in scripture over and over again, God's people knew to go to Him, especially when an enemy was pursuing them and they didn't know what to do. And just like them, we need to seek God's voice, His direction and His wisdom. And only when we study His word and pray, will we be able to clearly hear His voice. He wants to speak to you, but are you listening? Are you doing what it takes to have a clear connection so that no static (distractions) will plug up your spiritual ears? Or are you just letting things and people fill your ears with a lot of junk?

A couple of weeks ago, one of our praise team members left our church out of nowhere. I won't go into details, but for me, it was a total shock. No one saw it coming. It was really devastating to me and I took it pretty hard. I could barely sleep all night. I found out about it on Saturday night, right before I had to lead worship on Sunday.

Sunday came, and I had a couple of songs to lead. Well, my mind was still discombobulated from the news I had received the night before, so I forgot the words to the songs I was leading, and before I could even begin to sing the second song, the tears just began to come. I couldn't help it. I was a mess. I just needed to breathe and regain my composure. I finally got through the song. It was the last song on the worship set.

Once the song was over, I told the musicians to stop playing. I don't know why, but I was led to start singing the old hymn, How Great Thou Art. As soon as I began singing that song, there was a shift in the atmosphere. People began to stand up and rejoice. Then, I started singing another old hymn, Amazing Grace. God's spirit just began to fill the church and I could feel the burden lifting off of not just me, but others in the congregation. All because my spirit was open to His voice.

A lot of times we have our own plan, or agenda, and we have everything all mapped out of how we want our lives to go. We have this perfect little plan for our lives, and heaven forbid if anything messes it up. And to top it off, we never thought to pray and ask God, "What is your will? What do you want me to do?" I wonder how many times we would have made better decisions in our lives, if we had just prayed first, and then waited for God's answer, instead of rushing to do something to make us feel good.

In order to hear God's voice, we must first put ourselves in a position to hear His voice. First of all, you can't expect to know His will without reading His word. His will is His word understood. It's more than just reading His word, but it's getting an understanding of His word. Sometimes you have to turn off the chatter and get alone with God. You can't hear Him because there is too much noise. The noise of busyness, the phone and social media.

In 1 Kings 19, Elijah ran away to hide from Jezebel after she had pronounced a death threat on his life. Elijah had just had her 450 prophets of Baal killed, so needless to say, she wasn't very happy about that. And she showed it by sending her messenger to give Elijah his death notice. And like any one of us would've done, Elijah got scared and left town. He found a cave and spent the night there. While he was there, he got a visitation from the Lord.

> "The LORD said, "Go out and stand on the mountain in the presence of the LORD, for the LORD is about to pass by." Then a great and powerful wind tore the mountains apart and shattered the rocks before the LORD, but the LORD was not in the wind. After the wind there was an earthquake, but the LORD was not in the earthquake. After the earthquake came a fire, but the LORD was not in the fire. And after the fire came a gentle whisper. When Elijah heard it, he pulled his cloak over his face and went out and

stood at the mouth of the cave. Then a voice said to him, "What are you doing here, Elijah?" (1 Kings 19:11-13, NIV)

That gentle whisper mentioned above is called a still small voice in the King James. You would think that as big and powerful as God is, He would choose to speak through a strong wind, an earthquake or a fire. But not our heavenly Father. He's gentle and loving. He chose instead to speak in a gentle whisper.

What is God trying to tell you? Maybe He's trying to tell you to slow down. You're so busy doing this and doing that, that you don't have any time for Him. Maybe He's trying to tell you to forgive that loved one that hurt you so bad, because that unforgiveness you've been carrying around for a while now is choking the life out of you. Maybe He's trying to tell you to get your body in shape so that you can live a good long, healthy life.

One weekend, Albert and I got away for a couple of days. It was HEAVENLY, to say the least. We stayed at this beautiful bed and breakfast. We arrived on a Thursday and the other guests weren't going to be arriving until Friday. We had the whole house to ourselves. The rooms were furnished with lovely antique furniture. The owner had a lot of antique knives and swords, which Albert played with, like a kid in a toy store, while I took pictures of him.

After the owner showed us around, he gave us freedom to explore and do whatever we liked. It felt so good to be away, even for just a couple of days. You see, this was the first time we were away without our children, or any other family members or friends. Albert has a habit of inviting other people to go on our vacations with us, but we won't even go there. That's for a different book.

Albert was tired after the long drive there, and it was getting late. After he went to bed, I took a nice long bath in the jacuzzi tub. I felt like I was at a retreat, with nothing to do but relax. As I was sitting there, Holy Spirit began to enlighten my understanding of the word "retreat" and what it means. Retreat means to turn back and regroup. It's the act of "withdrawing".

We withdrew from the hustle and bustle of work and the world, to just breathe. We were secluded in this house off the road, in the woods and by a lake. The scenery couldn't have been more serene.

As I was sitting there in the tub, I felt such peace. Sometimes we're so busy that we don't know to just stop, retreat, and breathe. So when we finally do that, we feel like, "Why don't I do this more often?" It felt so good to just sit there and breathe, not having to worry about work, ministry, kids, or anything else.

What comes to my mind is a car with a dead battery. Have you ever driven a vehicle with an old battery, and you know it's getting old because the car won't crank and you need someone to give you a "jump"? Well, like a car battery, we can get tired and weary, walking around feeling overworked and overwhelmed. That's because we need a jump. We need to be refreshed and rejuvenated. It's okay to retreat, to withdraw and get alone. It's during those quiet times when He speaks to us and renews our strength and gives us peace that passes understanding.

God is always speaking. If He hasn't spoken anything to you lately, maybe it's because you haven't taken the time to just sit and listen. Get alone with our Daddy God and let Him speak to you. Whatever you need, it's in His presence.

Seven

IT'S NOT ALL ABOUT YOU

Look not every man on his own things, but every man also on the things of others. Let this mind be in you, which was also in Christ Jesus: And being found in fashion as a man, he humbled himself, and became obedient unto death, even the death of the cross. Wherefore God also hath highly exalted him, and given him a name which is above every name:
Philippians 2:4-5, 8-9

After I began writing this book, the Lord began to show me His purpose for my life more clearly. I began to have aspirations that I didn't have before I started writing. I didn't even want to write this book. I guess I had become complacent or settled, whatever you want to call it. But, then, God began to show me, "There's more I have for you." Then, along with this book, He began to put a greater desire within me to record music, and He began downloading songs into my spirit.

He's also showing me about the power of sowing into others. What you help make happen for others, God will make happen for you. In other words, we have to serve each other. Your blessing will not only come from sowing financially into your church, but sowing your time and resources into other people to aid them in achieving their dreams and goals. You are called to be a servant first.

Many of us don't want to hear that. We love going into a business establishment, and having others wait on us hand and foot, especially in restaurants. There's nothing like going into a restaurant, sitting down, and have someone come and ask you, "May I take your order, please?" You put in your order and you don't have to lift a finger, (except to grasp the spoon or fork to lift the food from the plate to your mouth). Your waiter or waitress brings out everything to you and places it right there in front of you for you to dig in. All you had to do was tell them what you wanted, and they gave it to you, exactly how you wanted it (at least most of the time).

Well, sorry to bust your bubble, but you weren't put on this planet for everyone to serve you. Part of the purpose for you being born is not just to serve God, but it is also to serve others. It doesn't just have to be monetarily, but maybe someone is going through a difficult time and just needs a word of encouragement, someone to tell them, "You're gonna make it." Or, maybe He does want you to sow monetarily into someone's life. Whatever it is, you have something to give.

What have you done lately to be a blessing to someone else? We live in a society in which everyone wants to be served, but few of us actually want to be the one doing the serving.

My favorite book in the Bible is Ruth. Ruth was the epitome of a servant. After her husband died, she left her hometown to go to a foreign city to live with her mother-in-law, Naomi, even though Ruth's husband was dead. Naomi told her to go back home, but Ruth adamantly refused. I love her famous words of determination, "Intreat me not to leave thee, or to return from following after thee: for whither thou goest, I will go; and where thou lodgest, I will lodge: thy people shall be my people, and thy God my God:" (Ruth 1:16).

By all means, Ruth had every right to leave Naomi and go live her own life. Naomi's son who was Ruth's husband, was dead. They didn't have any children, either. Ruth was young and could have let Naomi go back home while she stayed in her home town, remarried and perhaps had children and lived happily ever after. But Ruth was "steadfastly minded" (Ruth 1:18). She was determined that she was not going to leave Naomi's side.

In the next scene, Naomi and Ruth arrived back in Naomi's hometown. They have no money, so Ruth has to find a job to make provisions for herself and her mother-in-law. The book of Ruth tells us that it was the season for the barley harvest.

In those days, they didn't have welfare and government assistance. Unlike our welfare system today, back then, even if you were poor, you still had to work if you wanted to have food. The poor people had to pick up the leftover grain that was left on purpose for this very reason, so that they could eat.

Day after day, Ruth went to work so that she and Naomi could eat. She served Naomi, not looking for anything in return.

One day, while Ruth was picking grain, the owner of the field in which she was working, Boaz, noticed her. He just happened to be a close relative of Naomi's. Boaz was kind to Ruth and took notice of the way she cared for her mother-in-law.

According to Jewish law, the nearest of kin had the right to marry a woman after the death of her husband. Naomi had a relative that was closer in relation than Boaz, though, but he didn't want to marry Ruth. So, guess what? Boaz married her, and he was more than happy to do so.

Ruth wasn't looking for a husband. She just wanted to take care of Naomi. But in her serving, God blessed her.

She married Boaz and didn't have to worry about food, a place to live, or anything else for that matter.

We shouldn't serve to get something in return. Sometimes we need to be reminded that it's not all about us. Living a full life, a life of purpose, involves serving others with our time and our resources. And then God, in His faithfulness, will reward us when we serve with a pure heart. Ecclesiastes 11:1 says, "Cast your bread upon the waters, For you will find it after many days (NKJV). I like the way The Message Bible puts it, "Be generous: Invest in acts of charity. Charity yields high returns."

When you invest in God by serving others, you can't lose. It's a win-win situation. Not only is the person you're serving being blessed, but you should also walk away with a good feeling knowing that you were a blessing to someone else and that you're fulfilling God's Word that tells us to love our neighbors as ourselves. Nothing but blessing comes from our obedience. You can't lose when you live life His way.

Step Three

Get In Position

Eight

POSITION YOURSELF

> *Listen, King Jehoshaphat and all who live in Judah and Jerusalem! This is what the LORD says to you: 'Do not be afraid or discouraged because of this vast army. For the battle is not yours, but God's. Tomorrow march down against them. They will be climbing up by the Pass of Ziz, and you will find them at the end of the gorge in the Desert of Jeruel. You will not have to fight this battle. Take up your positions; stand firm and see the deliverance the LORD will give you, Judah and Jerusalem. Do not be afraid; do not be discouraged. Go out to face them tomorrow, and the LORD will be with you.'*
> *2 Chronicles 20:15-17*

My favorite chapter in the whole Bible is 2 Chronicles 20, which after I proofread this book, I seem to be talking a lot about this Bible passage in the chapters ahead. So, be forewarned.

Second Chronicles 20 talks about King Jehoshaphat and his enemies coming to attack him and the people of Judah. When Jehoshaphat got wind of the Moabites and the Ammonites coming after him, he started shaking in his boots. It was a natural response. Most of us would've reacted the same way.

So, Jehoshaphat set his face to seek the Lord and he called a corporate fast. And Jehoshaphat and all the people came together to seek the Lord's help. While they were praying and seeking the Lord, God's spirit came upon Jahaziel, a Levite, and he began to prophesy the above passage.

I love it when he said, "Take up your positions." And that's what I want to encourage you to do. Take up your position. Position yourself. We've become so lackadaisical, that we've forgotten who we are. We've forgotten that we are children of the King.

There's an old song we used to sing at my grandfather's church, "I shall not, I shall not be moved. I shall not, I shall not be moved. Just like a tree that's planted by the waters, I shall not be moved." It's one of those old school gospel songs, so you don't hear it that often anymore. We've stopped singing that song, and now we're being tossed to and fro and moving every which way. We have moved out of position.

So, how do you get back in position? First, you do it by realizing who God is. The Bible tells us He's our rock, our fortress, our Lord, our King, our life, our healer, our provider, our way maker, our miracle worker, our deliverer, our daddy. He's all these things and more. He knows who He is, but do we know who He is? He's love. If we knew that, we wouldn't fear. We wouldn't worry. First John 4:18 says, "There is no fear in love. But perfect love drives out fear, because fear has to do with punishment. The one who fears is not made perfect in love."

Notice that it says, "There is no fear in love." If God is love (1 John 4:8), then what this is really saying is, there is no fear in God, when you trust Him. There's no room for worry, when you trust Him. You don't have to doubt, when you trust Him.

So, what am I trying to say? Get in God! Position yourself in God! For too long the enemy has moved you out of your position. Stand up and get back in your position. Position yourself, stand still and see the salvation of the Lord!

We're into social media such as Facebook, Instagram and Twitter. But we fail to get into God. We spend hours on these media outlets, and get caught up in trying to keep up with everybody's business, instead of being about our Father's business. He wants us to be about His business. I'm not saying that those media outlets are wrong, even I get on Facebook every now and then. But when it gets to the point that our issues or other people's issues on the internet is consuming all our time, it's time to make a change.

"How do I do change," you may ask. One day at a time. We're all given the same 24 hours in a day. How much of that time do you spend in prayer, in the Word? Not nearly enough, for sure. What if I told you, your health depends on it? Your job depends on it. Your marriage depends on it. The health of your children depends on it. That promotion that you've been praying for depends on it. If we knew how vital it was to spend time in God's presence, most of us wouldn't have any problem setting aside a few minutes a day to spend time with God.

And, then, there are some of us who won't pray or study God's Word until tragedy hits. Then, we're on our knees in desperation crying out to God, feeling like all hope is lost, like we're about to lose our minds. Nobody has to tell you to pray then. Why do we let it get to that point, when all we have to do is go to God? Why? Because we're human. I'll admit that.

Even I get so caught up in life that I can go a whole day without giving Him any of my time. But whenever I'm going through something, I lose my appetite for food, and gain an appetite for God.

When we feast on what's on the news and what arrives in the mail…or what negative thought patterns keep reoccurring, it should be no surprise that fear, anxiety, and sadness show up in our lives. Our Father has an alternate menu for the child of God:

a mainstay of hearty meals on the Word of God seasoned with prayer.[2]

Sometimes the Lord allows things to happen just to get us back in position. But what a tragedy it is to be going through the hardest trial in your life, and you still can't find your way back to your position, that position of faith, of hope, of healing, of restoration, of joy, of peace. That is your position. And only when we try to do things our way, do we actually lose our way.

And before you know it, we're in this tsunami called life that has us tossed here and there. But be encouraged, my friend. It's not over. It's not over till God says it's over. Tragedy comes, and tragedy goes, but it's God who is always there, no matter what. When you can't find your BFF (Best Friend Forever), God is there. When you're going through the worst storm of your life, God is there. When you don't know what to do, God is there. Oh, praise God for his faithfulness! When I'm feeling faithless, he's still faithful. I can't help but give Him glory. He's always there. So why are you worried?

Every day, there's news about tragic events happening all over the world. And if you let it, it can really get you down. But that's when we have to be like David when he said in Psalm 121:1 & 2, "I will lift up mine eyes unto the hills, from whence cometh my help. My help comes from the LORD, Who made heaven and earth." Many times, we're too busy looking at the wrong things, instead of looking to Him. He's saying, "Yoo-hoo! I'm right here!" And yes, He patiently waits for us to get our stuff together and realize, "I'm nothing without you, Lord."

I remember when my children were very small. My son was four so he was able to walk, but my daughter was only two, so I put her in the shopping cart while I shopped at Meijer. I'm busy looking for a loaf of wheat bread (or something), so of course, I'm not paying attention when my son decides he'll walk away and venture out on his own. So, needless to say, when I turned to look for him, he was gone. Well, for you parents out there, I can't tell you enough how frightened I was after a few seconds of looking for him. I just started panicking as I was looking everywhere for him, calling his name, "Albert! Albert!"

And then out of nowhere, there he was, standing right there in front of me. I wanted to yell at him and scold him, and tell him that he better not EVER do that again. But I was just so happy that I found him, all I could do was throw my arms around him.

I believe that's how it is with God sometimes. We get caught up with the cares of life, having our eyes on everything (and everyone) but Him, that we begin to feel a loss, an emptiness, and a void that only He can fill. And He's just waiting for us to call Him. Matthew 11:28 says,

"Come to me, all you who are weary and burdened, and I will give you rest" (NIV)

Mmmmm, that sounds good, doesn't it? REST. I sure could use some right about now. But I'm talking about physical rest. But when it comes to God, He doesn't only give us physical rest, but mental rest. Rest for your mind, and for your soul. He will not only give you rest from your will and your way of doing things, but He will also give you the ability and faith to trust in His will and His way. Don't you know that when you do things His way, life would be so much easier?

Trust Him. He's got your back. Some of you are right on the edge of losing hope, and you're thinking, "If God doesn't work this situation out in my life, I don't know what I'll do."

Picture this very familiar movie scene, if you will, but just imagine it's you. You're hanging on the edge of a cliff and your fingers are slipping, one by one. You can't hold on for much longer, and if someone doesn't come quickly, you're going to fall off that cliff. But, all of a sudden, you see this person standing there, reaching down to take you by the hand and lift you up. And when you're finally standing on two feet again, all you can do is wrap your arms around that person and just pour out your gratitude upon them, telling them, "Thank you," over and over again.

That's what God is saying now, "Reach out to me. Come to me and let me give you rest. You tried it your way, now try it my way." What a beautiful place in which to be. Picture Him wrapping His loving arms around you, holding you. Can you feel His arms wrapped around you? Doesn't it feel good? That's what He wants to do for you every day. All you have to do is go to Him. Position yourself in His presence through prayer and His Word. Seek Him. Desire Him. Pursue Him. And He'll do the rest.

SPEAK TO IT!

That evening, Jesus said to his disciples, "Let's cross to the east side." So they left the crowd, and his disciples started across the lake with him in the boat. Some other boats followed along. Suddenly a windstorm struck the lake. Waves started splashing into the boat, and it was about to sink. Jesus was in the back of the boat with his head on a pillow, and he was asleep. His disciples woke him and said, "Teacher, don't you care that we're about to drown?" Jesus got up and ordered the wind and the waves to be quiet. The wind stopped, and everything was calm. Jesus asked his disciples, "Why were you afraid? Don't you have any faith?" Now they were more afraid than ever and said to each other, "Who is this? Even the wind and the waves obey him!"
Mark 4: 35-41, CEV

Jesus was asleep on a boat with his disciples, when a tumultuous storm arose. Of course, the disciples got scared and began to cry out to Jesus saying, "Teacher, don't you care if we drown?"

Notice that the first words he spoke were not to his disciples, but they were aimed at the storm. He spoke to the storm.

Many of us are speaking to the wrong things, and to the wrong people. Most of us would be so much better off if we stopped talking to some folks about all our business, and start talking to God first. And then, talk to your storm.

Luke 10:19 says, (and this is Jesus speaking to his disciples), "Behold, I give unto you power to tread on serpents and scorpions, and over all the power of the enemy: and nothing shall by any means hurt you." I just love the way King James puts it, "NOTHING SHALL BY ANY MEANS HURT YOU."

Do you believe that? Well, you should. You see, your enemy is not your boyfriend or girlfriend, not your husband or wife, not your kids, or your boss. Your enemy is the devil. The Bible tells us that he only has one job (or three, depending on how you look at it), to steal, to kill and to destroy. He doesn't care about your marriage, your family, your career, your house or the car you drive. He's after your soul, plain and simple. And he'll use whatever gets your fancy or whatever it takes to get you to move out of your position, whether it's divorce, death of loved one, or the loss of a job.

"Well, these are some pretty major things," you may say. And yes, you're right, they are. But there is absolutely nothing that God can't bring you through. Speak to your marriage! Speak to your finances! Speak to that depression! Speak to that sickness! Speak to that spirit of divorce, lack and fear and command it to go back to the pit of hell from whence it came, in Jesus's Name! It's not God's will for your home to be divided, for you to suffer lack orbe depressed. It's not His will for you to worry and be afraid.

Earlier, I referenced 2 Chronicles 20, when Jahaziel told the people to "not be afraid, nor be dismayed by reason of that great multitude." Here it was, three of Jehoshaphat's enemy nations joined together to make war against him, out of nowhere. I guess they had nothing better to do than mess with the people of God. The people of Judah are settled in the Promised Land, minding their own business, enjoying life, enjoying their families. And BOOM! Here comes trouble! Don't you just hate it when that happens?

In my first book, In the Midst of the Storm, I tell my story of how God blessed me and kept me standing in spite of temporarily losing Albert to a 16-year prison sentence, leaving me with two toddlers to raise on my own.

You see, I grew up in a loving two-parent home, and never had to go without. And then I was very blessed to have a loving husband, two beautiful healthy children, living in a nice home in a good neighborhood, where you didn't have to worry about gangs or crime. I was a stay-at-home mom, and I was just loving life.

Then all of a sudden, my BOOM! came. Albert went to prison. I had to get on government assistance and move back home to live with my parents. I lost my home, my car, and everything I owned. At that moment in my life, I became confused and unsure about a lot of things, but one thing—my faith. Quitting was not an option for me, no matter how bad it looked.

Sometimes, life, or stuff, just happens, and there's nothing you can do about it. Or is there? It's time for us to stop being bullied by the enemy. I made up my mind that I would no longer accept his lies and just be quiet. God has given us weapons, some of which are outlined in Ephesians 6, what's known as the whole armor of God.

He gave us these weapons to fight our enemy. First Peter 5:9 says, "Your enemy the devil prowls around like a roaring lion looking for someone to devour."

We have an enemy. That part is clear. Ephesians 6: 12-13 says, "For our struggle is not against flesh and blood, but against the rulers, against the authorities, against the powers of this dark world and against the spiritual forces of evil in the heavenly realms. Therefore put on the full armor of God, so that when the day of evil comes, you may be able to stand your ground, and after you have done everything, to stand."

Hear that? God is saying, "Stand your ground! You are more than a conqueror!"

"Well, how do I stand my ground," you may ask. By using your weapons. One of the weapons in Ephesians 6 is the sword of the spirit—the Word of God. You can't be silent. You have to declare His Word. In order to have victory in your life, being silent is NOT an option.

Find His promises in His word and memorize them. Then, when the enemy comes in with his lies and his attacks, you will be ARMED AND DANGEROUS! It's hard to stay down and depressed when you're speaking God's promises, over and over.

James 4:7 says, "Submit yourselves, then, to God. Resist the devil, and he will flee from you." Then, Isaiah 59:19 says, "When the enemy shall come in like a flood, the Spirit of the Lord shall lift up a standard against him."

Open up your mouth! No matter what you're going through, or will go through, God is bigger than your problem.

Job 22:28 says, "You will also decree a thing, and it will be established for you; And light will shine on your ways." Proverbs 18:21 says, "Death and life are in the power of the tongue: and they that love it shall eat the fruit thereof." In other words, there is power in your words, especially the word of God.

I'm reminded of the story of Moses and Korah in Numbers 16. Korah didn't like it that Moses was God's chosen one to lead the Israelites to the Promised Land. So, he took it upon himself to begin a rebellion against Moses and Aaron, Moses' brother who was chosen to be the priest.

Well, Korah decided that he wanted to be the priest. He wanted to do Aaron's job. He wasn't content with just being one of the worship leaders, he had to be the pastor, too, so much so that he rallied all of the Israelites together to back him up. You know how some of us used to do it back in the day, before we got saved. When someone wanted to fight us, we had to go round up our girls, or our boys, so that we could double-team the enemy.

Well, needless to say, when Korah got the idea to round up his boys, God didn't like it, which is an understatement. He was so displeased that he just wanted to kill all the Israelites, with the exception of Moses and Aaron. And He would've done it if it wasn't for Moses interceding for them, and pleading with God. However, Korah wasn't so lucky. God used him as an example to show what happens when you rebel against the almighty God and His chosen ones.

And Moses said: 'By this you shall know that the LORD has sent me to do all these works, for I have not done them of my own will. If these men die naturally like all men, or if they are visited by the common fate of all men, then the LORD has not sent me. But if the LORD creates a new thing, and the earth opens its mouth and swallows them up with all that belongs to them, and they go down alive into the pit, then you will understand that these men have rejected the LORD.' Now it came to pass, as he finished speaking all these words, that the ground split apart under them, and the earth opened its mouth and swallowed them up, with their households and all the men with Korah, with all their goods. So they and all those with them went down alive into the pit; the earth closed over them, and they perished from among the assembly. (Numbers 16:28-31)

Moses spoke, and it came to pass. Of course Moses' words brought a death sentence to Korah and all his family. But just like Moses spoke death over his enemies, we have that same power to speak life over our situations, and death to the lies of the enemy.

Speak how you want your life to be. It doesn't matter what it looks like on the outside. God has the final say. But you must know what His Word says in order to declare it. Mark 11:23-24 says, "For verily I say unto you, That whoever shall say to this mountain, be removed, and be cast into the sea; and does not doubt in his heart, but believes that those things which he says shall come to pass; he will have whatever he says. Therefore I say to you, whatever you desire, when you pray, believe that you receive them, and you shall have them." God's word does not lie.

Let us look at David, when he came face-to-face with a giant, Goliath, in 1 Samuel 17. We know the story of King Saul and the Israelites at war against the Philistines, which from the looks of it, things were not going well for the Israelites. David's brothers were on the battle lines, afraid like the rest of the Israelites. One day David's father sent him to go check on his brothers. While David was there, he heard Goliath shouting threats to the Israelites, which he did daily. Everyone was afraid, except David. So, he decided to take matters into his own hands and presented himself before the king. I love these words that David says to King Saul in verses 34-37:

Your servant has been keeping his father's sheep. When a lion or a bear came and carried off a sheep from the flock, I went after it, struck it and rescued the sheep from its mouth. When it turned on me, I seized it by its hair, struck it and killed it. Your servant has killed both the lion and the bear; this uncircumcised Philistine will be like one of them, because he has defied the armies of the living God. The LORD who rescued me from the paw of the lion and the paw of the bear will rescue me from the hand of this Philistine.

Wow! What boldness! How could Saul say, "No" to that? He couldn't. So, he let David go fight Goliath, just as he asked.

Next, we see David face-to-face with Goliath. If you thought what David said to Saul was good, check out what he said to Goliath to his face in verses 45-47:

You come against me with sword and spear and javelin, but I come against you in the name of the LORD Almighty, the God of the armies of Israel, whom you have defied. This day the LORD will deliver you into my hands, and I'll strike you down and cut off your head. This very day I will give the carcasses of the Philistine army to the birds and the wild animals, and the whole world will know that there is a God in Israel. All those gathered here will know that it is not by sword or spear that the LORD saves; for the battle is the LORD's, and he will give all of you into our hands.

I do believe these are my favorite words in the whole Bible! Oh, how we need the tenacity and determination that David displayed here.

Open up your mouth and declare, "Devil, you can't have my life! You can't have my marriage! You can't have my children! You can't have my home! You can't have my money! And right now, I command you take your hands off me and off my mind! No weapon formed against me shall prosper! I am the righteousness of God and I give you notice that I will not back down! I will not give up! Greater is He who is in me than he who is in the world! I am more than a conqueror and I shall not be defeated!"

There is power in your tongue. Use it! Use the power with which God has already equipped you. We have weapons at our disposal and we're not using them. This is a disservice to God and the body of Christ.

While you're at it, there's someone else out there who needs your words. It's time for you to prophesy! You don't have to be a prophet to prophesy. There are different levels of prophecy. All of us can prophesy. To prophesy simply means to edify, exhort and comfort. So, you not only have the power to speak to your storm, but you have the power to speak life and victory into other peoples' lives as well. Don't allow the enemy to keep you silent another day. Prophesy!

Ten

THERE'S POWER IN YOUR PRAISE

Shout with joy to the LORD, all the earth!
Worship the LORD with gladness.
Come before him, singing with joy.
Acknowledge that the LORD is God!
He made us, and we are his.
We are his people, the sheep of his pasture.
Enter his gates with thanksgiving;
go into his courts with praise.
Give thanks to him and praise his name.
For the LORD is good.
His unfailing love continues forever,
and his faithfulness continues to each generation.
Psalm 100, NLT

I've been a worship leader for almost 17 years now and it still baffles me how hard it is to get people to praise God sometimes. When I lead worship, I use verses like the one above, thinking, "Maybe if the people knew what the Word says about worship, they would do it." But, that doesn't work.

I thought that if people really knew the value of their worship, they would do it. Psalm 8:2 says, "Out of the mouth of babes and sucklings hast thou ordained strength because of thine enemies, that thou mightest still the enemy and the avenger."

I just received a new revelation about this verse, even now as I'm writing. And that is, if the praise from a little baby can silence the enemy, how much more can our praise silence the enemy, as people of God. A baby can't even form words, so how much more can our vast vocabulary be used to bring glory and honor to God and put an end to the works of the enemy.

Psalm 22:3 is an indication that God inhabits the praises of His people. In other words, wherever there is praise that is directed to our loving Father, He's there. He's in the midst. He yearns for our praises. He makes His home in our praise. And where the Lord is, there's no place, no room for the enemy.

Our praise is another spiritual weapon that defeats the devil. Our praise puts the devil on the run. That's why we need to know what our weapons are and use them. Ephesians 6:12 says "For we wrestle not against flesh and blood, but against principalities, against powers, against the rulers of the darkness of this world, against spiritual wickedness in high places." Then, 2 Corinthians 10:4 says, "For the weapons of our warfare are not carnal, but mighty through God to the pulling down of strong holds."

You can't fight the devil with guns and knives. You can't fight your enemy by telling them off on Facebook. Again, the enemy is not that person on Facebook who doesn't like you and so spreads rumors about you because they know it would make you angry. Your enemy, the devil, is a spiritual being. And, you have to fight spiritual beings with spiritual weapons.

Since we know that our praise invokes the Lord's presence, then we need to know that there's joy in His presence! Notice that it doesn't say there's sadness, depression, or worry in His presence. No! There's joy in His presence. And not only joy, but there's peace, love, healing, happiness, deliverance, wisdom, and the list goes on and on.

I believe that when we praise and worship God, angels are released to go to work on our behalf. Whenever you can praise God when everything in your life seems to be going wrong, that makes God happy. When He sees that we don't only praise Him when things are going good, but even when we're broke, busted and disgusted, and we still have praise on our lips, it touches His heart. It stirs something up in Him to move in our situation. And the devil knows that. He knows that as long as he can keep us discouraged, we won't want to praise God.

As long as the enemy can keep your mouth closed and keep you from giving God praise, no matter the situation, then he's won. Again, the devil isn't after your marriage, your children, or your finances. Along with your soul, he's after your praise.

As I spoke about earlier, it hurts my heart sometimes when I'm singing, and the people are just sitting there, looking at me. Looking hopeless. While I'm singing, I just think to myself, "If you would just open your mouth, lift your hands and give God some praise, how much better you would feel and how much better your life would be."

Our praise and our worship is an expression of our faith. Think about it. You really need faith to praise God when things are not so good. It's easier to have faith when everything's okay.

Acts 16 talks about the Apostle Paul and Silas being thrown in prison, another one of my favorite passages in the Bible. You'll have to read for yourselves why they were in prison, but I want to jump to my favorite part in verses 25 and 26:

> About midnight Paul and Silas were praying and singing praises to God, while the other prisoners listened. Suddenly a strong earthquake shook the jail to its foundations. The doors opened, and the chains fell from all the prisoners. (CEV)

Notice what happened when Paul and Silas were "praying and singing praises to God." Suddenly, the jail was shaken to its foundations, doors were opened and the chains were broken and literally fell to the ground. Instead of crying, "Woe is me," they chose to pray and sing praises to God. Look and look at the miraculous work God did.

We serve the same God that Paul and Silas served. He's the same yesterday, today and forever, and he is no respecter of persons. What He did for Paul and Silas, He will do the same for you.

When you praise God, He's able to turn your problem around just like that, and shake it to its foundation, until it's under your feet. He will open doors for you that no one can shut. He will bring you out of bondage and deliver you from the strongholds and chains that bind you. You may be thinking, "Are you for real? You mean that my praise can do all that?" These are the "pleasures forevermore" to which Psalm 16:11 alludes.

I need to point out that you don't have to wait until Sunday to give God praise. I've noticed that people who wait until Sunday to praise God, usually don't. If they haven't given God any praise during the week, they're not going to do it on Sunday either. They come to church and just sit there and watch the praise team praise God, like it's a show. It's usually hard to participate in something that you haven't done all week.

God is showing me how some of our hearts are far from Him. We come to church every Sunday out of ritual, but there's no relationship. There's no intimacy, no time spent with God in His presence. And as we get closer and closer to the Lord's second coming, it's only getting worse. Matthew 15:8 says, "These people honor me with their lips, but their hearts are far from me" (NIV). Second Timothy 3:2-5 says, "People will be lovers of themselves, lovers of money, boastful, proud, abusive, disobedient to their parents, ungrateful, unholy, without love, unforgiving, slanderous, without self-control, brutal, not lovers of the good, treacherous, rash, conceited, lovers of pleasure rather than lovers of God, having a form of godliness but denying its power. Turn away from such as these!"

Let's take another look at 2 Chronicles 20:21-23. God told King Jehoshaphat and the people of Judah to position themselves. How do you position yourself? You get in a position of praise and worship. Second Chronicles shows us what this position looks like:

> He appointed singers unto the LORD, and that should praise the beauty of holiness, as they went out before the army, and to say, Praise the LORD; for his mercy endureth forever. And

when they began to sing and to praise, the LORD set ambushments against the children of Ammon, Moab, and mount Seir, which were come against Judah; and they were smitten. For the children of Ammon and Moab stood up against the inhabitants of mount Seir, utterly to slay and destroy them: and when they had made an end of the inhabitants of Seir, every one helped to destroy another.

Wow! Do you see that? Again, another example of the power of our praise! This passage said that King Jehoshaphat put the singers in front. And as they praised God, the Lord set ambushments against the enemy. They believed that God would bring them out. Their praise was evidence of their faith. The ambushments were believed to be the angels of God. The enemies became so confused and discombobulated that they started to do away with each other, until there was not one person left on the enemies' side. By the time the army of Judah got to the battle site, all the Ammonites, Moabites and the inhabitants of Seir were dead. The only thing left for the people of Judah to do was take the spoils, which were the riches the enemies left behind. There was so much that it took them three days to gather it all up. Ephesians 3:20 says, "Now unto him that is able to do exceeding abundantly above all that we ask or think, according to the power that works in us." The people exercised the power of praise, and God did the exceeding, abundantly, above part.

There is power in your praise! Have you gotten ahold of that yet? Then, I'll say it again, THERE IS POWER IN YOUR PRAISE! You don't have to worry. You don't have to give up. You don't have to be depressed. All you have to do is praise God. Praise Him for He is so worthy!

We all have something to praise God for. Something that I would think about whenever the enemy wanted me to feel sorry for myself, is that there's someone who has it worse than I do. No matter how bad your situation or problem gets, there's always someone who has a worse problem or situation. We've heard the saying before, "Praise Him where you're at on the way to where you're going."

We waste time feeling sorry for ourselves, comparing ourselves to others, looking at what they have. God wants us to put our eyes on Him. Psalm 34:2 says, "With all my heart, I will praise the LORD. Let all who are helpless, listen and be glad" (CEV). God's word encourages us to be glad. He wants you happy.

You have something to praise God for, no matter what's wrong with your life, your marriage, your children, or your job. A lot of times we focus on the negative in everything, instead of what's good in our lives. Usually, there's more good than bad, if we would just open our eyes. Psalm 34:8 says, "Oh, taste and see that the LORD is good; Blessed is the man who trusts in Him" (NKJV). There's an old school saying that we would recite during testimony service back in the day, "When I think of the goodness of Jesus, and all that He has done. My soul cries out 'Hallelujah, praise God for saving me.'"

You may have cried today because nothing seems to be going right in your life, and you may feel hopeless. Just stop for a minute, sit down, and just write down or think about all the blessings in your life.

You see, this is what the enemy doesn't want you to do. He just wants you to have a pity party. There's a song that Wess Morgan sings titled, 'I Choose to Worship.' You have to make up your mind and decide that no matter what, I choose to worship my God. We have to be like our brother Job and say, "Though he slay me, yet will I trust in him…" (Job 13:15) Choose to say, "I will not give up. I will not give in. I know that God is going to bring some good out of this. And in the meantime, I will bless the Lord, and His praise will always be in my mouth."

Eleven

YOUR ANSWER IS IN HIS PRESENCE

For in the time of trouble He shall hide me in His pavilion: in the secret of His tabernacle shall He hide me; He shall set me up upon a rock.
Psalm 27:5

In 1 Kings 17, the Prophet Elijah has just pronounced a drought to King Ahab and the children of Israel. And because Ahab is a wicked king, God advised Elijah that it wouldn't be a good idea for him to hang around, because he may lose his life if he did. And God told Elijah exactly where to go until things cooled down a bit. He told him to hide by a brook which flows into the Jordan River, and that would be his source for water. Then, God told him that he would be fed by the ravens, and they were his source for food.

Once the brook dried up, God gave him another directive that led him to another food and water source. Needless to say, Elijah didn't have need for anything. He may have had some wants, but God definitely provided

Elijah with everything he needed, just like He does for us, His children.

Even though God can defeat our enemies, and rid us of all our troubles, sometimes He'll bring us to a place of desperation in our lives when we come to the realization that all we have is Him and that He's all we need.

God could've defeated King Ahab or anyone else who may have tried to come against His servant Elijah. But instead, He told him to go hide, "Leave and go across the Jordan River so you can hide near Cherith Creek," (1 Kings 17:3).

Why would God, the Sovereign Lord and creator of heaven and earth, tell one of His own to go and hide? That's where trust comes in. Trust in God's wisdom and that He knows what He's doing. Could it be perhaps, that God wanted to teach Elijah how to truly trust Him, how to depend on Him when no one else was around?

I remember when Albert went to prison and how so alone I felt, with just me and our two children, who I now had to take care of by myself. I remember feeling so devastated, like my world had just come crashing down all at once. It's the worst feeling I've ever felt before and since then. There's a saying that goes, "You never know God is all you need until God is all you've got."

God could've brought Albert home the first day we prayed, but He didn't. When I look back on that time, I now realize that God had Albert hidden—hidden behind bars. I know. It sounds crazy, right? But like I said earlier, our ways are not His ways, neither are our thoughts His thoughts. He knew how to get Albert's attention so that he would be totally sold out for God. And it worked.

What does it truly mean to be hidden in God? Before Albert went to prison, he was doing some things that I didn't know about and he didn't tell me about them until after he was incarcerated. I know that if I would've known what he was doing, I can't say that we would still be together today. It would have shattered me from the inside out. I believe with all my heart that God was hiding me as well. He kept Albert's activities hidden from me. And honestly, I'm glad He did.

God loves us so much, that He'll hide us. When our loved ones are doing things that would hurt us mentally and emotionally, whether it's our spouse or even our children, in order for us to maintain our peace and our sanity, God will keep it hidden from us. He sees the bigger picture down the road. He's our hiding place, our secret place.

Psalm 91:1 says, "He that dwelleth in the secret place of the most High shall abide under the shadow of the Almighty." When we're in the secret place, He keeps us safe from all harm. Elijah had to leave his friends and the comfort of his home to hide from King Ahab. But he had God, and God was all he needed.

My secret place is the bathtub. At the end of my work day, one of the best things that I like to do for myself is get alone with God in the tub. When I first get in the tub, I sit there, in quietness, and I just reflect on something that may have happened that day or the first thing that comes to my mind. Then, I'll turn on my worship music and let it play softly and I pray. Sometimes I'll begin praying in the spirit. Other times, I'll just start thanking God for His goodness. I'll also use different books with prayers in them and I pray the Word. If I have enough time, I'll sit there and I'll read a little. I can spend hours in my secret place.

Do you have a secret place? If not, you need to get one. Every child of God should have a secret place. There have been times I've been tired or stressed about something, and just not really in a good mood. I know that all I need is to spend some time with God and I'll be okay. It always does the trick. When I'm done spending time with Him, I feel refreshed and at peace. There's nothing like His presence. I feel blessed that He's taught me since way back when, the value of being in His presence. There are people who have been saved for years, and they don't know this. I call it one of the best kept secrets.

Do you know someone that every time you come across their path, they always have a sad story? They are always going through. When you see them coming, you almost want to turn and go the other way. The next time you see that person, you should tell them to find a secret hiding place and to get alone by themselves and just take some time to talk to God about their problems. There are some things that come only when we're alone with the Father, such as peace and relief from worry and anxiety. Worry and anxiety are derived from fear. It's so easy to worry, and the devil knows it. That's why the Word says, in Philippians 4:6, "Don't worry about anything; instead, pray about everything. Tell God what you need, and thank him for all he has done already."

I have addressed worry several times already up to this point. I believe that there's someone reading this right now who the devil torments with worry. And unless it's put in check and dealt with, worry can definitely be tormenting. My prayer for you is that you be set free NOW from that tormenting spirit. It is not of God and it is not okay! The Lord wants you free more than you want to be free. This is why I beg you to please find yourself a secret place and get alone with God. Tell Him what you need and cast all your cares on Him (1 Peter 5:7). He wants you to know right now that it's okay. He has it all in His hands. There's nothing too hard for Him.

Step Four

Embrace Your NEXT

Twelve

IT'S TIME TO DREAM AGAIN

And the Lord answered me, and said, "Write the vision, and make it plain…"
Habakkuk 2:2
Where there is no vision, the people perish…
Proverbs 29:18

Have you ever imagined yourself having more than what you have now? Doing more than what you're doing now? Have you ever had the feeling that there's something more? More than this?

At the writing of this book, I'm 46 years old. I believe that I have the ideal life that any woman would love to have. Even though I don't live in the biggest house or have all the money I could ever desire, I'm blessed. All of my needs are met, and most of my desires as well. So, my mind is not so much to have a lot of money, as it is to just walk out my purpose. There's a reason I was born. There's a reason you were born. And it's not just so you can grow, up, get a job, get married, have children, travel, and buy things.

God has so much more for you, outside of yourself. And it's not about fame or fortune. The world puts so much emphasis on those two things, that it's easy to get lost if you're not careful. While we need money to live and to have and do the finer things in life, some people tend to get lost in material gain and wealth.

Proverbs 6:9 says, "The mind of man plans his way, But the LORD directs his steps." More than making my name great, I just want "to do the will of Him who sent me." Those were Jesus' words in John 6:38. Nothing else matters if I'm outside of His will. I just want to be in His will.

What are your dreams and goals? There are so many books that have been written suggesting you write down your dreams and goals. The reason being is, when it seems like you'll never get there, like your dream will never be realized, you're able to go back to what you wrote down so that your faith can be strengthened to believe the impossible, but at the same time knowing that nothing is impossible for God

Problems, along with sickness or the death of a loved one have a way of taking your eyes off of your dreams. Problems such as job loss, eviction, or divorce just have a way of taking the very life out of you, almost to the point of hopelessness. That's why you need to dream.

Our dream is tied to our purpose. What is your purpose?

If you don't know your purpose, think about what you love to do more than anything. What is your passion? For me, it's singing. I love leading my church in praise and worship. Other than being a wife and mother, there's nothing else I get the greatest amount of joy from doing. So my dream has to do with recording an album someday and letting it be heard around the world, as it touches people, bringing healing and deliverance to the lost and the hurting. That's just one of my purposes for being born.

Each of us has a purpose. I believe that our purpose is connected to what we enjoy doing more than anything else in the world, our passion. As you walk in God's will and plan for your life, everything else will fall into place. Jeremiah 29:11 says, "For I know the plans I have for you," declares the LORD, "plans to prosper you and not to harm you, plans to give you hope and a future" (NIV).

God has a future for you, full of hope, prosperity and peace! That alone is something to get happy about! For some of us, before we write down our dreams, we need to first write down His promises. Once you know His promises, which is His Word, you will realize that there's nothing God can't do. And there's nothing that you can't accomplish through Him. There is purpose in you. And no matter how old you are, God has MORE for you!

What do you want out of life? What do you want to accomplish? Write it down and make it plain! Then, once you've written it down, it's time to start your research. Research people who have accomplished what you want to accomplish, find out what they did, and then do it.

Lisa Nichols, author of Abundance Now, said that one of the first steps she made to pursue her dream was she began to save money. She deposited checks into her savings account monthly and in the memo line of the check she wrote Funding My Dream.3 She did this for a number of years until she had saved $62,000 to go towards funding her dream.

I have adopted that concept and I currently deposit money into my bank account monthly to fund my dream. It's going to take money to market this book and to make a music recording, so I'm saving for it now. I then did a Google search on how to market my book. There are so many resources out there, you just have to take the time to do your homework.

It's a question of how bad do you want it? Some of us are content sitting on the sidelines watching someone else accomplish their dreams, because well, for us, it's just too hard. It's too much work and it takes too much time. It's easy to sit back and just be content with the way things are, because it's just too much work to change it.

It would be easy for me to just be content working for someone else, earning a nice salary until I retire. But God has given me this deep yearning for more. It's not just about me, but it's about purpose, which somehow makes this life full of possibilities, to get out of my comfort zone and just GO FOR IT! And that's what I want to ask of you. Why not go for it? What have you got to lose?

What is that dream you had years ago, but somehow it got lost along the way, and you just forgot about it? Write it down, and know that this time, NOTHING will keep you from walking in your purpose and realizing your dreams.

Once you write it down, see it and envision it coming to pass. Yes, I'm a firm believer of positive thinking or whatever you want to call it. See it as if it's already done. "For as a man thinks in his heart, so is he…" (Proverbs 23:7, NKJV).

> *Affirm it, visualize it, believe it, and it will actualize itself. Change your thoughts and you change your world.*[4]

Proverbs 18:16 says, "A man's gift makes room for him, and brings him before great men" (NKJV). Someone needs that gift that's inside of you. God has given you everything you need to live a comfortable life; now it's time for you to give back to the world the gifts that He's placed inside of you--and make money doing it, if you so desire. Yes, you heard me right. The Bible talks about money, and God wants you to have it.

Do you think that God gave you gifts and talents just for you to sit on? No! Absolutely not! They are for you to share with the world. Your future looks great, because His plans are to prosper you, spiritually and financially-- to give you hope and a future (Jeremiah 29:11). I'm ready!

The question is "Are you ready?"

Thirteen

INCREASE YOUR VALUE

The beginning of wisdom is this: Get wisdom. Though it cost all you have, get understanding.
Proverbs 4:7, NIV

Wisdom is "the soundness of an action or decision with regard to the application of experience, knowledge, and good judgment." Understanding means "comprehension."

More than anything, I seek to understand God's word. His word is his wisdom. The definition of wisdom is "the soundness of an action." Wisdom is the application of knowledge. You need to do more than just know something, but once you know, do you use what you know? Knowing a lot doesn't make you wise. Applying what you know makes you wise. You can know the Bible from cover to cover, but are you living it? Are you applying it to your life, in what you do and in what you say, and even in where you go?

When your decisions line up with the Word of God, heaven supports you.[5]

There are places that God wants to take you, but you don't yet possess the wisdom it takes to remain there. There are some things you've been praying for, and God has not yet granted you your desire, because you don't have the wisdom to maintain or keep it if He was to give it to you.

When you speak to people, you don't just want to have a good word, but you want to have a God word. But, in order for you to have knowledge and in order for you to speak with power and authority, you need wisdom. Wisdom that doesn't come from YouTube or Facebook, but wisdom from Holy Spirit. Having something meaningful to say requires knowing what's meaningful. You make yourself valuable as you increase in knowledge. Then, when you find yourself surrounded by others who no doubt have problems and issues and concerns of life, you will be their solution. In other words, you will be that channel that God will use to bring healing and deliverance to that individual(s).

When you obtain knowledge, understanding and wisdom, you become someone else's solution and your value to your family, friends, coworkers, and the world increases. Someone needs your gifts, your talents, and your wisdom. You have a purpose. You may not know what it is yet, but we all have a purpose. We all have gifts and talents. But using what you have takes wisdom.

What are you doing to hone your gifts, to make them better? Don't know? It all starts with wisdom. Only you have the power to increase your value. No one else can do it for you. We've heard the saying, "Knowledge is power!" But, actually, knowing is only a part of it. It's applying what you know. You can have all the knowledge in the world, but without application, it's really not doing you any good.

I'm always looking for ways to be a more effective worship leader. I read books and articles and I watch instructional videos. And then on Sunday morning, I apply what I've learned. Even during the week, I'm practicing the songs, I'm praying and fasting, I'm in the word, so that when I minister, I'm effective. Something that has become my motto lately is serving God with a spirit of excellence.

I have even started taking vocal lessons. I desire to have the vocal stamina and strength to do what God has called me to do. I'm 46 years old and I've sung in church since I was a little girl, but one thing I know I lack is technique, such as how long should I warm up my voice, and what I should or shouldn't eat and drink. Until recently, I didn't know that a singer or speaker is supposed to cool down their voice once they're done singing or speaking, in order to keep their voice in the best possible condition.

When I sing, I put my all into it, but at the same time, I don't want to strain and ruin my vocal cords causing long-term damage. I have the wisdom to know that no matter how long I've been singing, I don't know everything, so I'll seek out a professional. I'm determined that nothing will keep me from walking in my divine purpose and destiny, and you should be determined, as well.

You may enjoy singing, playing an instrument, speaking, cooking, etc. Some people even have the gift of cleaning. What are you doing to make yourself better at what you do? Have you ever thought about getting paid for what you enjoy doing? Well, you can. Yes, it takes work and diligence, but most of all, it takes wisdom. Obtaining wisdom takes time. You have to do the work, and while success may not come overnight, each day you're getting wisdom, you're one day closer to fulfilling your dreams. That may sound cliché, but it's possible. With God, anything is possible.

The illustration that comes to mind is the picture of someone wanting to build a house. We all know that before a house can be built, you need a plan, a blueprint of what you want the house to look like. Then, once you have a blueprint, you hire a carpenter or a company that's known for building homes.

We all know that that house isn't going to be built in one day, and if it is, you know like I do that you wouldn't live one day in that house, because we all know that building a home takes time, more than a day, more than a week, more than a month, and sometimes, more than a year. But the end result, if done right, is a beautiful new home!

Do you want a more fulfilling life for yourself, and don't know where to start? Get wisdom! In my reading, I've learned that one of the habits of successful and well-known people is that they read often. They know that knowledge, and the application of it, is power. As I said earlier, I'm reading more books now, along with the written word of God. You can't leave that out. It's God's word first! And everything else is second. A lot of the principles that you read in self-help books are taken from the word of God.

It's okay to want more out of life. Jesus said in His word that He came that we may "have life and have it more abundantly." It is God's will for you to live the abundant life. However, you have to seek Him first. It all goes back to God. But when you seek Him, like Matthew 6:33 says, "…all these things will be given to you as well." And even though the previous verses talk about food and clothing, you and I both know that God has SO much more that He wants to add to you. But you have to do your part. Proverbs 4:7 begins with, "Wisdom is the principal thing;

therefore get wisdom…" Principal means "main; first in order of importance." Wisdom is the main thing.

I also like the New Living Translation version, "Getting wisdom is the wisest thing you can do!" How many bad choices have you made in life, that if you would've had good sense and wisdom, you probably would've made a different choice?

Getting wisdom is more than just a way to fulfill your dreams or make more money. You need wisdom just to make the right decisions and to keep yourself from living a life of regrets. Granted, none of us are perfect. We all make mistakes once in a while and we learn from our mistakes. We can even gain wisdom from our mistakes. But if you've made the wrong choice over and over again, you need wisdom, especially if you keep making the same mistakes over and over again.

One of the reasons I'm writing this book is simple. I'm writing this book for YOU. I know that you want wisdom. I know that you want to do better and be better, or you wouldn't be reading this book.

I've probably said it over and over many times already, but you have a purpose to complete on this earth. God has a special plan for your life that he planned just for you. You are important to Him. You are valuable. You are worth His love.

Something else that I really enjoy doing is propelling people into their destiny. And that's another reason why I take the time to increase in knowledge, understanding and wisdom. Then, God enables me to use that wisdom to be someone's answer. And He wants to do the same for you.

Don't you want everything that God has for you? Then, I'll say it again. Get wisdom! Knowledge is all around us, on the internet, on CDs and DVDs and in books. You don't have an excuse! Don't put it off. It's time for you to walk in your divine purpose, fulfill your dreams that you've put on the shelf, and start possessing everything that God has for you. Say "hello" to your future. You were made for this! You're ready for this!

Fourteen

WISE STEWARDSHIP

And the Lord said, Who then is that faithful and wise steward, whom his lord shall make ruler over his household, to give them their portion of meat in due season? Blessed is that servant, whom his lord when he cometh shall find so doing.
Luke 12:41-43

One day I was listening to a podcast from a well-known worship music artist. She was talking about stewarding the presence of God and all that entails. She used that term a lot, "steward." It's not a term you hear a lot, so even though I have a good idea of what it means, I decided to look up the definition. A simple definition of "steward" means 'to manage or look after.' The word "steward" is used a lot in the Bible to refer to someone, normally a servant, who has been given the responsibility of being in charge of their master's house and business affairs. Their job is to manage or look after the home, especially when the master is away.

God is our master and we are the servants that He has left in charge to steward His resources. When He comes back, will He find you being a good steward or a bad steward? Luke 16:10-12 says, "Whoever can be trusted with very little can also be trusted with much, and whoever is dishonest with very little will also be dishonest with much. So if you have not been trustworthy in handling worldly wealth, who will trust you with true riches? And if you have not been trustworthy with someone else's property, who will give you property of your own?" (NIV)

Are you a wise steward of what God has entrusted to you--your talents, your money, your time, and your relationships? Or do you sit on your talents and hide them? Do you spend money frivolously? Do you waste time? Do you mistreat your friends and family members and take them for granted?

You want more out of life, right? But what are you doing with what God has already given to you? How do you steward, or manage, your possessions?

Take your home, for instance. Is it clean? What about your car? Is it clean? Or is it dirty with a lot of food crumbs and garbage on the inside? When was the last time you deposited some money in the bank? When was the last time you balanced your checkbook? Do you pay your bills on time? Do you constantly overspend and never have any money left over until your next paycheck? How do you treat people? Are you mean or kind?

Do you spend all your time on Facebook and Netflix, and before you know it, the whole day or evening has gone by with nothing left to show for it? What about your relationships? Do you spend time with your spouse or your children? Do you check on those who mean the most to you?

A lot of good questions, huh? It's a lot to think about. We want success and prosperity, but have you been faithful with what you already have?

Your time, your money, and your talents are valuable resources that God has given to you. You only have one life to live here on earth as we know it now. What are you doing with it? You may be thinking, "Wow! There are a lot of things that need work in my life! Where do I start?"

The best way to start is to start small, with baby steps. It's never good to take on a large project all at once. So, let's start small and work our way to the bigger issues.

You may be a person who isn't very good at keeping your home organized. There are papers everywhere; clothes on the floor that need to be hung in the closet, etc. The first thing to do is to get some of those plastic drawers that they sell at Meijer. Or, if you can't afford them, find some old shoe boxes. Then, collect all the papers and just start going through each sheet, one by one. Keep the important papers that you need and throw away the old papers that you don't need. Have a 'keep' pile and a 'junk' pile.

The same thing goes for all those clothes lying on your floor. Some of them, you can't even fit into anymore, if truth be told. If that's the case, make two separate piles for those, too, one to keep and one to give to charity or a friend who would love to have them.

After your house is clean, start with the car next. If your car is already clean, start with the checkbook. Or better yet, do something nice for your spouse or spend some time with your children. Then, work on the checkbook.

Being a wise steward also has to do with priorities. What are your priorities? Your hair and nails, or your family? Now, before you close the book because you don't like what I just said, give me a chance to clarify. As a woman, I know that we love getting our hair and nails done. That's not a bad thing. It only becomes a problem when that's your first priority. It's okay to check your priorities from time to time. Sometimes, we allow ourselves to get out of balance. Then, before you know it, your whole life is out of whack.

Now, remember that you don't have to put everything in order all at once. For some of those things I mentioned above, it's going to take more time for certain things than it will for others, which is why I said to start small. Start with that thing that's the easiest and work your way up to the more challenging things.

After I had worked all week, I used to be able spend hours on my couch watching old classic movies on the Turner Classic Movie (TCM) channel, my favorite channel. However, once God put this desire in me and a revelation of the things He has in store for me that I have yet to experience, my desire is not to sit on the couch for hours watching movies, but to spend my time more wisely. My desire for movies has shifted into a desire for knowledge and wisdom. I'm like a sponge, soaking up the words off the pages of the books that I read. I'm obtaining knowledge on marketing and the necessary steps that I need to take to move me into the next season God has planned for my life. At the same time, I'm saving money and nurturing my relationships with Albert and my children. I'm enjoying using my gifts for the kingdom and am enjoying the journey along the way.

I use my time and I spend my money wisely. I've never been a person who likes to waste time or spend money on things I don't need. I feel very strongly about three things: my time, my money and my food. Yes, even food. These are three things that God gives us and that I value highly. If you waste a lot of time, a lot of money, and a lot of food, you need to do some reevaluating of your values and pray and ask God to help you be a wise steward of these blessings.

When you become a faithful and wise steward of what God has already given you, you set yourself up for more and bigger and better.

Another saying that comes to mind is, "Blossom where you're planted." Maybe you're already a wise steward of your possessions, relationships and the blessings that God has placed in your life, but you're wondering, "I've been praying and seeking God and doing everything I know to do. So, when will my time come?" Only God knows the answer to that, but the best thing you can do now is to not quit. Keep doing everything you know to do, and do it well. You, and no one else, are the steward of your life. Blossom where you're at, at this stage of life that you're in now. Enjoy your journey.

Many times we're in such a hurry to get to the destination, that we don't enjoy the trip. Everything that God has for you will come to you in due time, in your "due season." Each of us has our due season. The problem is not knowing when it's due. But as long as you continue to remain faithful in the small things, your due season is just around the corner. Galatians 6:9 says, "And let us not be weary in well doing: for in due season we shall reap, if we faint not."

I cannot stress it enough when I say, DON'T GIVE UP! You may be thinking, "Boy! I have lot to work on." Don't be discouraged. Take your time. Whatever you do, don't quit.

Fifteen

WALK INTO YOUR NEXT

So shall my word be that goes forth out of my mouth: it shall not return unto me void, but it shall accomplish that which I please, and it shall prosper in the thing whereto I sent it.
Isaiah 55:11

In Matthew 9, beginning at verse 27, two blind men were following Jesus, begging Him to have mercy on them, as they wanted to be healed from their blindness. Jesus asked them, "Do you believe that I am able to do this? They answered saying, "Yes, Lord." Then He touched their eyes, saying, "According to your faith be it done to you." And their eyes were opened.

I ask you today, "Do you believe?" God desires so much to take us from glory to glory, from one level of faith to another. But we're stuck on yesterday's blessing. We've gotten comfortable.

God wants to give you an increase of His blessings, power and anointing. He may tell you to go left, but you'll go right instead, because that's what you're used to doing. Change is hard. I hear the Spirit saying, "Arise out of your complacency." This is your season. God has so much more for you than this. Do you believe it? You've prayed and asked God for some things and now you're waiting. What are you doing while you wait?

I recall a time when God wanted to bless me with a better, high paying job. I was working as an executive assistant for one of the vice-presidents at the University of Toledo. The job was a little fast-paced, but nothing that I couldn't handle, or so I thought. I later learned that my boss had a different perspective. Come to find out, she wasn't happy with my performance. I even sat down with her and tried to get an understanding of the disrespect that I could feel she was displaying towards me. I tried to do better in meeting her expectations, but she was done. She gave me 90 days to find another position. And since hindsight is always 20/20, that was the best thing she could have ever done for me. So, I began my search for a new position.

To make a long story short, I was hired to work in a far less stressful environment, with a $5,000 increase in my income! God had something better for me, but He knew that I wouldn't have started looking for a new position on my own, so He allowed my current position to get uncomfortable for me to the point that I had no choice, but to move. My season ended at the first place, and it was time for my new season to begin someplace else. It was time for my NEXT. And I've never been happier.

Earlier, in Chapter 2, I talked about Albert being released from prison and being evicted from the state of Michigan. Again, that was one of the best things that could've happened to us. It was preparation for our NEXT.

God knows what's best for us. We always think we know what's best, but we don't. That's why Proverbs 3:5-6 says, "Trust in the LORD with all thine heart; and lean not unto thine own understanding. In all thy ways acknowledge him, and he shall direct thy paths." He knows our end from our beginning. All we have to do is believe. Then, when He tells us to move, we need to move.

God wants to give you the desires of your heart. His word does not lie. He said it and He will perform it. It will not return to Him empty, or void. He has so much for you, but you have to do more than ask. You have to ACT. James 2:20 says, "Faith without works is dead."

Are you feeling uncomfortable yet? Did God give you a directive that you have yet to do, because you're either too comfortable or too afraid?

We all know the story about the Israelites. They were so comfortable being slaves, making bricks, depending on the Egyptians for their food and livelihood, that when it was time for them to possess the Promised Land, they failed.

Here it is, after 400 years of slavery, the deliverer, Moses, had finally come. Moses led them out of Egypt, through the Red Sea that swallowed up the Egyptian soldiers that were on their trail; God was a pillar of cloud by day and pillar of fire by night. He gave them water out of rocks and fed them food from heaven; neither their clothes nor their shoes wore out. They were so close to the Promised Land, the land of milk and honey. But they never possessed it. After Moses sent in the 12 spies to scope everything out in Canaan, they said, "We can't attack those people! They're too strong for us! They're big and we're small!"(Numbers 13)

And so there they remained, in the wilderness for 40 years, until they all died, except Caleb and Joshua, the only two men who had the faith to believe that they could overtake the Canaanites and take what belonged to them. It's really one of the saddest stories in the Bible, to be so close to what you've been praying for all along, then when it's finally here, you allow fear to keep you from taking hold of it. And you fail to act.

But be encouraged! It's not too late. As long as you're still alive and breathing, it's never too late. That's a lie from the devil. You can do anything you want to do. Philippians 4:13 says "I can do all things through Christ who strengthens me" (NKJV). Arise from your complacency. You have come too far to give up now.

I love the story in Matthew 15:21-28 that talks about a woman whose daughter was demon-possessed. A Canaanite woman came to Jesus begging him to heal her daughter. First, he basically ignored her and didn't say anything. But she could've cared less. This was her daughter we're talking about. And as a parent, you will almost do anything for your child.

So, the woman just kept on following Jesus and shouting until he finally answered her saying that he was only sent to the people of Israel. Some people would've just given up then, but not this woman. She wasn't giving up that easily. She got closer to him and knelt down, begging, "Please help me, Lord!" Then, Jesus replied, "It isn't right to take food away from children and feed it to dogs." You would think that after being called a dog, either you walk away, or there's going to be a fight. But neither happened. And you have to love this woman for her quick reply, "Lord, that's true, but even dogs get the crumbs that fall from their owner's table."

Talk about resilience. This woman was not going to leave until she got what she came for. Jesus answered her, "Dear woman, you really do have a lot of faith, and you will be given what you want." At that moment her daughter was healed.

This Canaanite woman had such faith and determination; she wasn't going to take "No" for an answer. Lord, I want that. When things get hard, it's the devil's job to discourage us to the point that we want to give up and quit. It's easier to quit than it is to fight or to act. "Nope, this is just too hard. I'll just go over there into my little corner and cry, thank you very much!"

Isn't that how we feel sometimes? We'd rather go stick our head in a wall until the storm passes over. Oh, if it was only that easy. But, no. We have to fight. You have to go after that thing that you've been praying for and don't stop until you have it.

What do you want? What have you asked God for, but have yet to see it materialize? I love what John 15:7 says, "But if you remain in me and my words remain in you, you may ask for anything you want, and it will be granted!" (NLT) Do you see that? He said, anything. But let's not forget the precondition.

When a student starts college, they have to take what's called "core classes", before they can begin prerequisite classes, or the classes that are related to their program of study or major. The core classes have nothing to do with their major, but you can't get your degree until the core classes are done; classes like History, Chemistry, Art, etc. These are classes you'll probably never use in the real world or in your career. Nevertheless, these classes are necessary in order to fulfill the ultimate goal--to get a degree.

In John 15:7, Jesus is saying, "In order to get what you want, abide in me and let my word abide in you." Why? Because it's the Word that will bring you through. And when our eyes are upon Him, there's nothing we can't do. There's nothing He won't give us.

The Canaanite woman wasn't deterred. She knew what she came for, and she wasn't leaving until she got it. God wants us to be the same way. Pick those dreams back up. God gave Joseph dreams, and despite the pit, the slavery and the prison, he held on to those dreams, and in God's time, they came to pass.

Know that what God has promised, He is well able to perform, for He is faithful (Romans 4:21; Hebrews 10:23). No, it's not going to always be easy. But it's worth it. Let your faith come alive right now. Believe for the incredible, the impossible. There is nothing too hard for God. He is so good! And if you don't receive it as soon as you ask for it, know that it's on the way. Why? Because you didn't stop believing. It's not up to you to know how He's going to do it. Just know that it's already done.

Conclusion

As of the publication of this book, I still have yet to receive some things that I've been believing God to do for me. In the meantime, He's commissioned me to write this book.

When I first started writing, after I wrote a few pages, I just stopped, because I didn't feel like doing it. Then, one Monday evening when I was at church in prayer, my pastor prayed for me and began to prophesy through the Holy Spirit's leading. He told me how God is giving me a new book to write. Then, I tried to use some lame excuse of why I stopped writing. I said that I don't just want to give a good word, but I want to give a God Word. My pastor then said that I didn't have to worry about that because when I sit down to write, the Lord would just give me the words to say. I knew that. So, I couldn't even use that for an excuse. God already knew my excuses. When I think back on it, it's really kind of funny. Don't think you're hiding anything from God. He already knows. He knows your excuses, too.

He's told you to do something, and you still haven't done it. He told me to ask you, "What are you waiting for?" It's easier to say you have faith, than it is to get up and do what needs to be done to go after what you desire. But I know you know this. Faith without works is dead, D-E-A-D, dead. Your wishing for it isn't going to make it happen. Are you doing everything He's told you to do up to this point? If not, why not?

If this book does nothing else, I pray that it causes a fire to rise up inside of you that cannot be quenched. That, for those of you who know me personally, it will make you say, "If Dorenthea can do it, then I can do it!" That you will get to the place that you won't settle, but that you will arise and possess everything that God has for you.

WALK INTO YOUR NEXT!

Endnotes

1. [Arise&Shine]. (2013, September 6). Myles Munroe: 10 Principles for Leadership Development [Video File]. Retrieved from https://youtu.be/ DZ2uWAxrVQ.

2. Sheila Walsh, I'm Not Wonder Woman, But God Made Me Wonderful! (Nashville: Thomas Nelson, Inc., 2006), 181.

3. Lisa Nichols & Janet Switzer, Abundance Now: Amplify Your Life & Achieve Prosperity Today (New York: HarperCollins Publishers, 2016).

4. Norman Vincent Peale, The Power of Positive Thinking: A Practical Guide to Mastering the Problems of Everyday Living (New Jersey: Prentice-Hall, Inc., 1952).

5. Creflo Dollar, Eight Steps to Create the Life You Want: The Anatomy of a Successful Life (New York: FaithWords Hatchette Book Group, 2008), 6.

Made in the USA
Lexington, KY
16 March 2018